IT'S SCIENCE!

Food

IT'S SCIENCE!

Food

Sally Hewitt

W

FRANKLIN WATTS
LONDON•SYDNEY

First published in 1999 by Franklin Watts
This edition published in 2001

Franklin Watts
96 Leonard Street
London EC2A 4XD

Franklin Watts Australia
56 O'Riordan Street
Alexandria, Sydney
NSW 2015

Series editor: Rachel Cooke
Designer: Mo Choy
Picture research: Sue Mennell
Photography: Ray Moller unless otherwise acknowledged
Series consultant: Sally Nanknivell-Aston

ISBN 0 7496 4275 0

Dewey Decimal Classification Number 614.3

A CIP catalogue record for this book is available from the
British Library.

Printed in Malaysia

Acknowledgements:
Cover: Steve Shott; Bruce Coleman pp. 14tl (Harald Lange), 16tm (Gerald Cubitt),
26bl (Kevin Rushby); FLPA pp. 26tl (Philip Perry), 26tr (D. P. Wilson);
Holt Studios International pp. 7l (Nigel Cattlin), 14tm (Nigel Cattlin), 14tr (Nigel Cattlin)
14bl (Nigel Cattlin), 16tr (Gordon Roberts), 17tl (Nigel Cattlin), 17tr (Nigel Cattlin);
Images Colour Library pp. 15tl, 25tr; Planet Earth Pictures p. 7m (Martin Rugner),
16br (Peter J. Oxford); Telegraph Colour Library p. 7r (Frank Krahmer).
Thanks, too, to our models: Shauna Morris, Natimi & Shalika Black-Heaven,
Jack Mitchell and Erin Bhogal.

Contents

Food for life

Plants, animals and everything that is alive, including you, need food. Food gives your body the **energy** to work, keep warm and stay healthy.

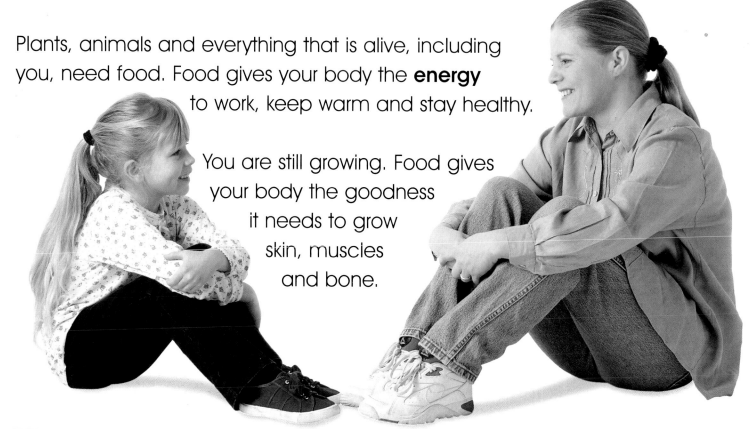

You are still growing. Food gives your body the goodness it needs to grow skin, muscles and bone.

After a night's sleep or when you have been playing or working hard and you haven't eaten for a while, you feel hungry. Your **stomach** is empty and you need food.

TRY IT OUT!

Start the day with a good breakfast. It will give you the energy you need for all the things you want to do before lunch.

Plants make their own food. They change the heat energy in sunlight into food in their green leaves.

Rabbits eat plants like grass and vegetables. They are hunted and eaten by meat eaters.

Foxes are meat eaters. They hunt and eat other animals like rabbits that eat plants.

Follow this **food chain**. You can see that even though foxes don't eat plants they would soon go hungry if there were no plants for rabbits to eat.

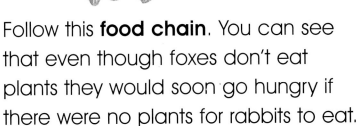 **THINK ABOUT IT!**

Where do you think people would fit in to a food chain?

Eating

You have to eat food to get the energy and goodness from it.

Before you start eating, the smell of food you like makes your mouth water as it fills with **saliva**.

You chew your food into small pieces. Saliva helps your food to slip down when you swallow and starts to break up the food even more.

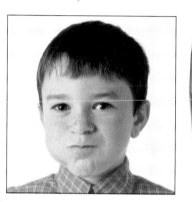

You need strong, healthy teeth to eat your food. Food left around your teeth can damage them, particularly if it is sugary – so brush your teeth every morning and evening to keep them clean.

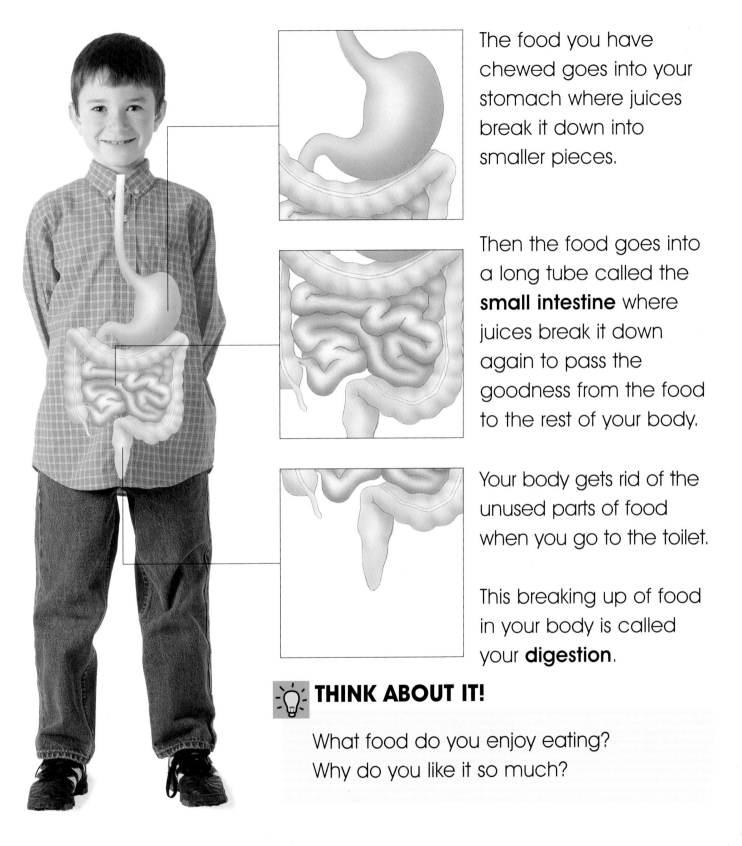

The food you have chewed goes into your stomach where juices break it down into smaller pieces.

Then the food goes into a long tube called the **small intestine** where juices break it down again to pass the goodness from the food to the rest of your body.

Your body gets rid of the unused parts of food when you go to the toilet.

This breaking up of food in your body is called your **digestion**.

THINK ABOUT IT!

What food do you enjoy eating?
Why do you like it so much?

Good food

There are four main groups of food. Eating a good mixture of them every day helps to keep you strong and healthy.

You only need a small amount of **fat** for warmth and energy.

The **protein** in foods like meat, fish, eggs, cheese and nuts helps your body to grow and to get better. You should have some protein in each meal.

Lots of fresh fruit and vegetables will give you the **nutrients**, such as **vitamins**, you need to keep every part of your body healthy.

The **carbohydrates** in this group of food give you energy. Plenty of bread, pasta, rice or potatoes will help to keep you going.

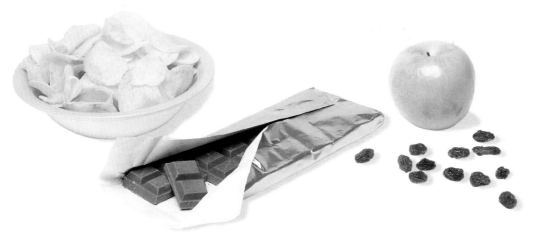

Snacks like crisps and chocolate are full of salt and sugar and it is not good to eat too much of them. Try an apple and some raisins for a snack instead.

Your body also needs a lot of water to work properly, so don't forget to drink water as well as eat good food.

TRY IT OUT!

Plan a meal you would like to eat choosing food from all the four groups. Is it a healthy meal?

Is this meal full of the goodness you need?

Fruit and vegetables

The fruit and vegetables we eat are all parts of plants. Fruit is the part of a plant that holds the **seeds**.

Sweet pineapples, bananas and melons are all fruit, so are apples and pears.

Some fruits are not so sweet, such as tomatoes and courgettes. We often call these fruits vegetables, but can you spot the seeds that show they are fruit?

Vitamins and **minerals** are found in most foods but fruit and vegetables give us the most. Oranges are full of vitamin C. It helps to keep your skin healthy and to make you better when you are unwell.

The vegetables we eat can come from all different parts of a plant.

Broccoli is a kind of flower.

We eat the leaves of a lettuce.

Crunchy celery is a stalk.

Carrots are roots growing under the earth.

 THINK ABOUT IT!

What parts of the plants do you think potatoes, cauliflower, cabbage, onions and spinach come from?

 TRY IT OUT!

Ask an adult to help you wash and slice some fresh fruit or vegetables to make a fruit salad or a vegetable salad that is good to eat.

13

Grains

Grains are seeds. Grains we can eat are used to make a lot of our food. You probably eat some kind of grain every day.

This is barley.

This is maize.

These are oats.

Wheat is a kind of grain that gives food for millions of people all over the world. It is grown in huge fields that stretch as far as you can see.

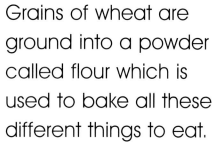
Grains of wheat are ground into a powder called flour which is used to bake all these different things to eat.

Rice is another important grain. It grows in hot places underwater in flooded paddy fields.

The food made from grains is full of **fibre**. We sometimes call it **roughage**. There is roughage in fruit and vegetables, too.

Roughage helps all the food you eat to pass through your body more easily.

Can you tell which of these foods are good to eat for roughage?

👁 **LOOK AGAIN**

Look again at page 10 to find what group of food grains belong to.

15

Food from animals

Some of the food we eat comes from animals. It gives us protein, fat, minerals and vitamins.

Cattle, sheep and pigs are farmed for meat.

Fishermen drop nets into the sea and pull up huge catches of fish. Sometimes fish are frozen on board ship as soon as they are caught to keep them fresh.

💡 THINK ABOUT IT!

Some people choose not to eat meat and fish. Look at page 10. What could you have for protein instead of meat and fish?

Chickens give us eggs as well as meat.

Dairy cows are farmed for their milk. Milk is used to make all these different kinds of food.

 TRY IT OUT!

Make some pancakes.
Sieve 110 grammes of plain flour into a bowl. Gradually whisk in 2 eggs and 275 ml of a mixture of milk and water.
Ask an adult to help you to cook the pancakes.
You can eat your pancakes with syrup, orange juice, cream cheese or anything you choose.

Pizza

Pizza is full of energy and nutrients. Do you know where all the different kinds of food, or **ingredients**, used to make pizza come from?

A tomato is a fruit that turns red in the sunshine. Tomato sauce is made from crushed tomatoes.

Olives are the fruit of an olive tree. Olive oil is made from pressed olives.

Cheese is made from milk that comes from dairy cows.

Basil is a herb which is a type of plant. Its leaves have a strong smell and taste.

Dough is made from flour, yeast and water.

Yeast is a kind of fungus that is good for us. It makes the dough of the pizza base rise.

Salami sausage is made from meat that has been ground up and forced into a sausage skin.

👁 LOOK AGAIN

Look again at page 10. What food groups do the ingredients of this pizza come from?

✋ TRY IT OUT!

Make a pizza collage.
Draw round a plate and cut out a circle of card. Paint on red tomato sauce. Cut strips of yellow tissue paper for grated cheese. Cut circles of coloured paper for salami sausage. Make prints from mushrooms and peppers and cut them out. Stick the things you have made on your pizza.

What else could you put on your pizza? Ask an adult to help you make a real pizza using the toppings you have chosen.

Look, smell and taste

You use your senses to decide if food is good to eat. Food that looks good makes us want to eat it. Food that looks colourful and fresh is good for you. Food that is old and stale doesn't look tasty. It has lost some of its goodness and can make you ill.

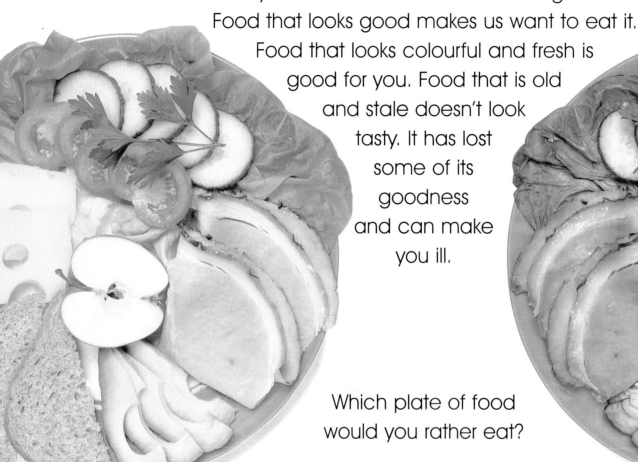

Which plate of food would you rather eat?

 TRY IT OUT!

Make a meal that looks good to eat from food that you don't need to cook. How can you make it look even more delicious?

Uncooked food that smells nasty could be going bad. It might make you ill if you eat it.

The smell of good food cooking helps to make you hungry. Just the smell can make your mouth water. This means your mouth is getting ready to eat the food.

Your tongue can only detect salty, sweet, sour or bitter tastes. Has Anna just tasted something sweet or sour?

Salt, pepper, herbs and spices are used to give flavour to food. You only need to add a little to food as they have a very strong taste.

Chillies can make food taste very hot!

Fresh and clean

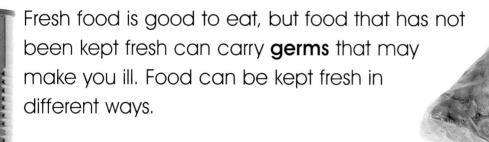

Fresh food is good to eat, but food that has not been kept fresh can carry **germs** that may make you ill. Food can be kept fresh in different ways.

Fresh food like green vegetables and fish can be kept in the refrigerator for several days. If you freeze it, you can keep it for several months.

Dried food keeps until water is added.

Food in tins keeps until the tin is opened and air is let in.

Often food you buy has a 'use by' date on its packaging. It tells you how long you can safely keep the food before eating it.

USE BY
1/1/2002

Good cooks make sure their food is fresh and everything they use is clean. Cooks often wear a hat to keep their hair out of the food.

Always wash your hands. They may have germs on them that could get into the food.

Wash your cooking utensils and dry them with a clean cloth.

 **LOOK AGAIN**

Not all food has a date on it. Look at pages 20 and 21 to find other ways you can tell when food is not fresh.

 **TRY IT OUT!**

Make a poster to put in the kitchen to remind everyone about using fresh food and keeping clean.

Wash your hands

Cooking

Most of the food we eat is cooked – it is heated until it changes. Raw food has not been cooked at all.

Cooking food makes it easier to chew and to break up inside your body. The heat also kills off germs and makes the food safer to eat.

Some foods taste much better cooked. Some are more tasty if they are raw.

THINK ABOUT IT!

Which of these foods could we eat raw?
What other food can you eat raw?

The heat from a cooker, a barbecue or a fire is used for cooking food. We can use the heat to boil food in water, grill it, fry it in fat or oil or bake it in an oven.

We fry or grill sausages. They look very different when they have been cooked.

Boiling, scrambling or frying are different ways of cooking eggs. How was this egg cooked?

 **LOOK AGAIN**

Look again at page 15 to see how boiling rice changes it. Does it get bigger or smaller?

Bread is baked in the oven. Flour, water and yeast are the ingredients needed for making bread. Look how cooking changes bread dough.

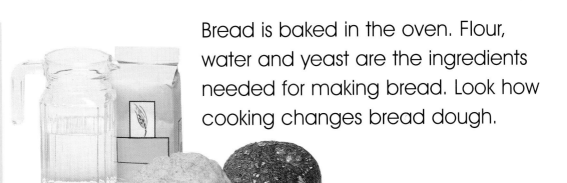

Shopping

Do you like shopping for food? The food you buy comes from all over the world.

Bananas grow where it is hot and wet. They have a long way to travel to the shop where you buy them. They are picked when they are still green. By the time they reach the shops, they are ripe and ready to eat.

The cod in your fish fingers is caught in cold seas and frozen on board ship to keep it fresh for you to buy.

Most of the tea we drink comes from India where tea leaves are picked, dried and put into packets.

 TRY IT OUT!

Look at the packaging and labels of the food in your cupboard or refrigerator and see if they tell you where it comes from.

Tea

The food from this shopping basket has been sorted into packets, tins, fresh food and frozen food.

Now it has been sorted into food made from grains, fruit and vegetables, protein and fat.

THINK ABOUT IT!

What other ways can you think of for sorting this basket of food? Try sorting the food you buy into different groups next time you go shopping.

27

Useful words

Carbohydrates Carbohydrates are found in some foods, such as bread and pasta. They help to give you the energy you need each day.

Digestion The ways your body breaks down and uses the food you eat.

Energy Energy is what people, animals and machines need to give them the power to do work. Your energy comes from food.

Fat There is fat in food such as meat and butter. Your body can store fat and use it slowly to give you energy.

Fibre Fibre is a part of plants, including food such as grains and vegetables. It helps food to pass through your body easily.

Food chain A food chain is the name given to the way plants and animals are linked together by what they eat.

Germs Germs are too tiny to see with our eyes. They carry diseases that can make you feel ill. There may be germs in food that is not kept fresh.

Grains The seeds of plants such as wheat, barley and maize are called grain. Grains can be dried and ground into flour. Bread and pasta are made from grains.

Ingredients Ingredients are the different foods we put together when we cook. For example, the ingredients for making a pancake are flour, eggs, milk and water.

Minerals Tiny amounts of minerals are found in food. They are an important part of the goodness in food that helps to keep you healthy.

Nutrients Nutrients are the goodness in food that you need to stay healthy.

Protein Protein in food such as fish, meat, eggs and cheese helps to build up strong bones and muscles in your body and helps it to heal.

Roughage Roughage is another word for fibre in food. It helps food to pass easily through your body.

Saliva Saliva is a liquid made in your mouth that helps your food to slip down when you swallow. It starts to break up the food before it reaches your stomach.

Seeds Plants grow from seeds. A seed contains a new plant and its store of food.

Small intestine Food goes into your small intestine from your stomach. It is a long tube where juices continue to break down food from your stomach.

Stomach When you eat, your food goes into your stomach where juices break it down into very small pieces.

Vitamins Vitamins are part of the goodness in food. They help to keep every part of your body healthy.

Yeast Yeast is a tiny fungus used in baking. (Fungi are a group of living things, including mushrooms.) A mixture of water, sugar and yeast added to bread dough makes it rise.

Index

About this book

Children are natural scientists. They learn by touching and feeling, noticing, asking questions and trying things out for themselves. The books in the It's Science! series are designed for the way children learn. Familiar objects are used as starting points for further learning. Food starts by looking at why we need food and explores the different aspects of food that relate to science.

Each double page spread introduces a new topic, such as cooking food. Information is given, questions asked and activities suggested that encourage children to make discoveries and develop new ideas for themselves. Look out for these panels throughout the book:

TRY IT OUT! indicates a simple activity, using safe materials, that proves or explores a point.
THINK ABOUT IT! indicates a question inspired by the information on the page but which points the reader to areas not covered by the book.
LOOK AGAIN introduces a cross-referencing activity which links themes and facts through the book.

Encourage children not to take the familiar world for granted. Point things out, ask questions and enjoy making scientific discoveries together.